The Flying Change

The Flying Change

Poems by HENRY TAYLOR

Louisiana State University Press
Baton Rouge and London
1985

86 87 88 89 / 8 7 6 5

LIBRARY OF CONGRESS CATALOGING IN PUBLICATION DATA

Taylor, Henry, 1942–
   The flying change.

   I. Title.
PS3570.A93F59   1985   811'.54   85-11295
ISBN 0-8071-1263-1
ISBN 0-8071-1264-X (pbk.)

Publication of this book has been supported by a grant from the National Endowment for the Arts in Washington, D.C., a federal agency.

The author is grateful to the National Endowment for the Arts, a federal agency, for a Creative Writing Fellowship during which a considerable portion of this collection was written.

The editors of the following journals, in which most of these poems first appeared, are thanked for their hospitality to the poems, and for permission to reprint them here: *The Back Door, The Beloit Poetry Journal, Claymore, Desperado* (Folded Broadside, Unicorn Press, 1979), *Folio* (American University), *Gargoyle, Hampden-Sydney Poetry Review, The Hollins Critic, Into the Round Air* (Thistle Publications, 1977), *Light Year 84* (Bits Press, 1983), *Light Year 85* (Bits Press, 1984), *The Little Brown House: A Garland for Robert McGlynn* (Deerfield Press, 1984), Palaemon Press Broadside Series, #12, *Plainsong, Ploughshares, Southern Poetry Review, Southern Poetry: The Seventies* (Southern Poetry Review Press, 1977); *The Southern Review, The Virginia Quarterly Review, The Washington Dossier, The Washingtonian, The Washington Times, The Western Humanities Review,* and *Window.*

"Taking to the Woods" first appeared in *Poetry.*

For Frannie

Trying to say what I want you to know,
I am a spangled dancer, in bold tights
and sash, whose feet are nailed to the floor.
My hands and arms can weave their vague suggestions,

but not the leap toward your understanding.
Like a tree, stuck to the ground, I sway
and sigh; my fingers fall like leaves; and still
somehow you catch my drift, and dance around me.

Contents

I / Heartburn

Landscape with Tractor

How would it be if you took yourself off
to a house set well back from a dirt road,
with, say, three acres of grass bounded
by road, driveway, and vegetable garden?

Spring and summer you would mow the field,
not down to lawn, but with a bushhog,
every six weeks or so, just often enough
to give grass a chance, and keep weeds down.

And one day—call it August, hot, a storm
recently past, things green and growing a bit,
and you're mowing, with half your mind
on something you'd rather be doing, or did once.

Three rounds, and then on the straight
alongside the road, maybe three swaths in
from where you are now, you glimpse it. People
will toss all kinds of crap from their cars.

It's a clothing-store dummy, for God's sake.
Another two rounds, and you'll have to stop,
contend with it, at least pull it off to one side.
You keep going. Two rounds more, then down

off the tractor, and Christ! Not a dummy, a corpse.
The field tilts, whirls, then steadies as you run.
Telephone. Sirens. Two local doctors use pitchforks
to turn the body, some four days dead, and ripening.

And the cause of death no mystery: two bullet holes
in the breast of a well-dressed black woman
in perhaps her mid-thirties. They wrap her,
take her away. You take the rest of the day off.

Next day, you go back to the field, having
to mow over the damp dent in the tall grass
where bluebottle flies are still swirling,
but the bushhog disperses them, and all traces.

Weeks pass. You hear at the post office
that no one comes forward to say who she was.
Brought out from the city, they guess, and dumped
like a bag of beer cans. She was someone,

3

and now is no one, buried or burned
or dissected; but gone. And I ask you
again, how would it be? To go on with your life,
putting gas in the tractor, keeping down thistles,

and seeing, each time you pass that spot,
the form in the grass, the bright yellow skirt,
black shoes, the thing not quite like a face
whose gaze blasted past you at nothing

when the doctors heaved her over? To wonder,
from now on, what dope deal, betrayal,
or innocent refusal, brought her here,
and to know she will stay in that field till you die?

Somewhere Along the Way

You lean on a wire fence, looking across
a field of grain with a man you have stopped
to ask for directions. You are not lost.
You stopped here only so you could take a moment
to see whatever this old farmer sees
who crumbles heads of wheat between his palms.

Rust is lifting the red paint from his barn roof,
and earth hardens over the sunken arc
of his mower's iron wheel. All his sons
have grown and moved away, and the old woman
keeps herself in the parlor where the light
is always too weak to make shadows. He sniffs

at the grain in his hand, and cocks an ear
toward a dry tree ringing with cicadas.
There are people dying today, he says,
that never died before. He lifts an arm
and points, saying what you already knew
about the way you are trying to go;

you nod and thank him, and think of going on,
but only after you have stood and listened
a little while longer to the soft click
of the swaying grain heads soon to be cut,
and the low voice, edged with dim prophecy,
that settles down around you like the dust.

As on a Darkling Plain

The years pile up, but there rides with you still,
across old fields to which you have come back
to invent your home and cultivate the knack
of dying slowly, to contest your will
toward getting death behind you, to find a hill
where you can stop and let the reins go slack
and parse the dark swerve of the zodiac,
a face whose eyes find ways to hold you still.

They hold you now. You turn the chestnut mare
toward the next hill darkening to the west
and stop again. The eyes will sometimes change,
but they ride with you, glimmering and vast
as the sweet country you lost once, somewhere
between the Blue Ridge and the Wasatch Range.

Evening at Wolf Trap

Once, outside the theater's weathering walls,
we sat on the grass with wine and cheese,
French bread and fruit; and as we ate, our talk
was sometimes interrupted by a small crowd

farther down the hill, throwing a frisbee
and calling to each other in a language
none of us knew—Romance in origin,
possibly something South American.

With spectators' expertise we remarked
one woman's lack of control, another's grace,
and the accurate artistry of one small man
who set the frisbee spinning hard and straight

to rise a little on the wind, and pause,
then, like a drift of milkweed, settle down
so slowly toward a woman's outstretched hands
that in that moment all things ceased to age.

At last their circle closed; they drew together,
sat down, and in that mysterious language
sang old songs we almost thought we knew.
There was something in those hovering syllables

that might have been calling me to join them,
sit down and strike up a song of knives, or love,
their language lifting effortlessly from my tongue.
It was not that their happiness was more than mine,

but only my hearing something out of reach
that I will not need to try to find again.
I am satisfied to know that it was there,
floating in that dusk above an outstretched hand.

Cutting Torch

I wait between darkness and light, at the door
to a blackened machine shop, the noon parking lot
behind me, and squint into the gloom at a man

with a torch. He leans to his work, a strip
of steel marked with chalk, lowers the goggles
from their resting place on his forehead.

He eases the flame to one end of the chalk line.
A small spot turns red, and as droplets of metal
begin to shiver in the blast from the torch,

sparks fall and splash at his feet. All these years
he has studied the shapes flame can make;
he bores holes, works designs in sheet metal,

even joins, with melting rods of brass or steel,
what another time and purpose put asunder.
You get used to the burned-out trouser cuffs,

he says, and hot drops of steel in your sleeve,
but no one gets quite good enough to remember,
always, which pieces are still too hot to pick up.

The Way It Sometimes Is

At times it is like watching a face you have just met,
trying to decide who it reminds you of—
no one, surely, whom you ever hated or loved,
but yes, somebody, somebody. You watch the face

as it turns and nods, showing you, at certain angles,
a curve of the lips or a lift of the eyebrow
that is exactly right, and still the lost face
eludes you. Now this face is talking, and you hear

a sound in the voice, the accent on certain words—
yes! a phrase . . . you barely recall sitting outside,
by a pool or a campfire, remarking
a peculiar, recurring expression. Two syllables,

wasn't it? Doorknob? Bathroom? Shawcross? What the hell
kind of word is shawcross? A name; not the right one.
A couple of syllables that could possibly be
a little like something you may once have heard.

So the talk drifts, and you drift, sneaking glances,
pounding your brain. Days later a face occurs to you,
and yes, there is a resemblance. That odd word, though,
or phrase, is gone. It must have been somebody else.

Yes, it's like that, at times; something is, maybe;
and there are days when you can almost say what it is.

Bathing in Lightning

Start the hot water running in the tub,
    arrange the book, the towel . . . I am snapped
out of myself as a slow splintering crash
    advances from the hills and rolls to rest

by my window. I think how lightning might
    smash among the pipes behind my walls, run
echoing through that buried jungle gym,
    emerging to impale me as it goes to ground.

Auroras flash at the faucets, fireballs roll
    around the room, the glowing walls; the water
trembles to receive me; now the heavy air
    lightens for the last time in this life,
    and I step in, lie back, and let it come.

Getting Himself Together
after Baudelaire's "Recueillement"

He takes his pain to the woods, to settle down.
Wanting the dark, he shuts the cabin door
while the town he left lies buried in thick air
he once breathed freely, watching others drown.
Back there, they run like cattle down a chute
to low at those lascivious marquees
or slobber over rubber novelties;
so he carries his pain here to shake it out
away from them. On the gray planks upstairs
old calendars are curling up like scrolls
until all he can see is the painted scene
of a mermaid combing starfish from her hair,
or a flyspecked sunset. Toward midnight he unrolls
his sleeping bag and beds down with his pain.

More Than One Way

As to the cat itself, traditionalists tend
to start with a dead one. Take a sharp knife
and cut rings at all four ankles, then half-ring the tail

on the underside. Open the belly from crotch
to throat, and peel the skin from the hind legs.
Punch a small hole above each second joint,

between tendon and bone, for the ends
of a ten-inch gambrel stick, tapered
toward its tips like a sailplane's wings.

Hang the whole business on a peg, head down,
at eye level. With two oak dowels, form a makeshift vise
to grip the base of the tail: as you pull, the tailbone

slips free like a leg being drawn from a stocking.
Coax the skin from the torso, slicing the stretching white
web of mesentery. The head, if you decide to try it,

takes patience. Cut to the end of the lower jaw,
hook your fingers deep in the incision,
and push with your thumbs on the skull.

Cut off the nose button from underneath,
and it will stay with the skin; but whatever care you take,
there are two shapeless holes where the eyes used to be.

If that goes too slowly, give up on the tail;
just chop it off. Forget the gambrel stick;
place one foot on the rear paws and snatch upward,

lifting the whole hide as you might lift
a shirt from a child. You can even make
a quick slice around the middle and pull both ways

at once, if all you are after is what is inside.
Traditional methods, however gently applied
to even the strongest of living subjects,

have predictable results. Think back now
to childhood: how you hung from a bar
by your hands, curled up and dived between your arms

and down lightly to touch earth with your toes,
then twirled back. There were times, at that
instant of liftoff, when you could see yourself

as if part of you stood to one side watching.
In such moments of grace, a cat might come to a move it awaits,
the right sound or look of love, out of its skin by way

of its eyes or breath, to put all its lives in your hands.
But if this happens often, you will come to count on it,
and begin to take pride in what you are merely given.

Should such error overtake you, do two things:
dull your knife on oak for a gambrel stick,
then whet it on stone toward the genuine task.

Shapes, Vanishings

1

Down a street in the town where I went
to high school twenty-odd years ago, by doorways
and shadows that change with the times, I walked
past a woman at whose glance I almost stopped cold,
almost to speak, to remind her of who I had been—
but walked on, not being certain it was she,
not knowing what I might find to say.
It wasn't quite the face I remembered, the years
being what they are, and I could have been wrong.

2

But that feeling of being stopped cold, stopped dead,
will not leave me, and I hark back
to the thing I remember her for, though God knows
how I could remind her of it now.
Well, one afternoon when I was fifteen
I sat in her class. She leaned on her desk,
facing us, the blackboard behind her arrayed
with geometrical figures—triangle, square,
pentagon, hexagon, et cetera. She pointed
and named them. "The five-sided figure," she said,
"is a polygon." So far so good, but then when she said,
"The six-sided one is a hexagon," I wanted things clear.
Three or more sides is *poly*, I knew, but five only
is *penta*, and said so; she denied it,
and I pressed the issue, I, with no grades
to speak of, a miserable average to stand on
with an Archimedean pole—no world to move,
either, just a fact to get straight, but she
would have none of it, saying at last, "Are you
contradicting me?"

3

A small thing to remember a teacher for. Since then,
I have thought about justice often enough
to have earned my uncertainty about what it is,
but one hard fact from that day has stayed with me:
If you're going to be a smartass, you have to be right,

and not just some of the time. "Are you
contradicting me?" she had said, and I stopped
breathing a moment, the burden of her words
pressing down through me hard and quick, the huge
weight of knowing I was right, and beaten. She
had me. "No, ma'am," I managed to say, wishing
I had the whole thing down on tape to play back
to the principal, wishing I were ten feet tall
and never mistaken, ever, about anything in this world,
wishing I were older, and long gone from there.

4

Now I am older, and long gone from there.
What sense in a grudge over something so small?
What use to forgive her for something
she wouldn't remember? Now students
face me as I stand at my desk, and the shoe
may yet find its way to the other foot,
if it hasn't already. I couldn't charge
thirty-five cents for all that I know
of geometry; what little I learned is gone now,
like a face looming up for a second out of years
that dissolve in the mind like a single summer.
Therefore,
if ever she almost stops me again,
I will walk on as I have done once already,
remembering how we failed each other,
knowing better than to blame anyone.

The House in the Road

Topping a rise one night on a narrow road
    across country I thought I knew,

I saw I was heading straight to the front
    of a big white clapboard house.

I slapped on the brakes and slowed down in time
    to hold the curve as it dipped away to the left,

ten yards from the front door. I made the turn
    and drove on, remembering that I have done

this same thing at this same place perhaps
    a hundred times in my life,

and that the house has been there longer
    than anyone now alive.

It still surprises me, being there like that,

and for a little while after I pass it
    I wonder how they live there.

Each night, headlights blaze at the windows,
    making furious shadows rake the walls;

tires cry on the curve, recover, and roll on,
    and everyone breathes easy again.

Or else they have been there a long time,
    and nothing has happened; over the years

they have forgotten that every night their being there
    makes someone sweat and wrestle the wheel;

the lights, and the shadows they cast on the walls,
    have come to mean the same thing, always.

Someone is driving by, that's all, on his way
    to the town up the road, or beyond;

that I have felt their peril and wished them well
    will never occur to them.

They go on about their business, thinking
no more of cars in the living room

than I, the next time I drive this way,
will be thinking of a house in the road.

Heartburn

It is not middle age,
you tell yourself, getting up
from the table without breathing too deeply,
lest breath stir the fire in your gut;
it's not crotchety digestion
flaring up after years of eating incautiously.
You've burned like this after dinner
since you were seventeen years old,

when they stood you in front
of a screen in a dark room,
and two men in green coats watched as radio-
active chalk drink swirled in the faint
light that picked out their gray faces.
But the thing gets harder to live with, and you spend more
ill-tempered time, these days, clawing
in the dark room for the tail end

of the pack of Rolaids
that must be somewhere, in one
of the tweed coats, maybe, that haven't been worn
for months, and you picture yourself
in a pith helmet, hacking trails
to the heart of the treacherous closet.
                                              So. Get up,
put on what comes to hand, and go
out, down the dark drive to the gate

where you lean and look out
over fields at the mountain
and beyond it to the soft dome of cloud-light
suspended above the city
some fifty miles away.
                                   Not far,
yet as bright as it looms, you remember that right here
a black cow has been lying dead
for weeks at the foot of the bank

below the drive, having
fallen down into the stream
when a section of the stone culvert caved in,
and the rock that pins her is bound

to weigh over a ton, so she'll
be there, pulsating with maggots, drawing the local
vermin out of the woods, until
someday the bones are clean enough

to pick up and ponder.
Dark as it is, you walk down
to her now, catch a whiff of her, and for some
reason the moil in your stomach
subsides. It is only farm death,
the sound and smell you've known all your life.
Still, you indulge
for a few moments the notion
that one day you too might end up

with your head in a creek,
under a rock, crushed into
the earth you once found other ways of wishing
to merge with.
Listen. The night wind
is not strong, but now it catches
a dead leaf just right, whips it against a twig, making
it sound like a train in a dream,
clicking out some message in code,

as if such things could speak
to your heart; but that leaf is
as dead as the cow, and the cow is about
the deadest thing you can think of
in this vicinity. Turn, then,
and guess for a little while at the houselights tricked out
on the side of the mountain, where
people may be watching tv,

or thinking, as you do,
that the time may be coming
for some sort of change, and the thought fans the flame
in your belly, your grip tightens
on the rail of the gate.
Now tears,
as you look up at the sky, make the stars seem to speak
with more meaning than they possess,
and they say that whatever you

burn for—some plausible
answers to the momentous
questions you can't even think of, or only
an uncomplicated evening
in bed with someone you have no
true claim to—you almost had hold of it once, but now
you recall it imperfectly.
If you need a change, just stand here,

by God, and you'll get it.
So turn once again, back up
the driveway, thinking, as lately you've come to,
that you can still make a wrong step
on rough ground, in the dark, and not
quite cripple yourself. Porchlights, left on to show the way
home, shine right in your eyes, and you
can't see a thing, but you'll get there.

II / Barbed Wire

Taking to the Woods

Clearing brush away
is the mean part of working up firewood from these
cut-off treetops—a chaotic souvenir
of the doubtful covenant I made the day
I marked a dozen white oak trees
and sold them for veneer.

There might be more in this
of character or courage if it were need that drove
my weekly trials in this little wood,
but this is amateur thrift, a middle-class
labor as much for solitude
as for a well-stocked stove.

For more than safety's sake,
therefore, I take a break to light up and daydream,
and as the chainsaw ticks and cools, I smoke
my way back to an hour spent years ago,
when I knelt above a shallow stream—
the scanty overflow

from the springhouse at my back.
The ache of holding still dwindled away to less
than the absent-minded effort that has carved
these grooves between my eyebrows; on the surface
oarlocked water-striders swerved
above the scribbled black

shadows minnows made
on rippled mud below their bright formations,
and a dragonfly, the green-eyed snakedoctor
with wings out of old histories of aviation,
backed and filled down a stair of nectar-
scent toward a jewelweed

and struck a brittle stillness
like the spell the wood boss broke when he touched my hand
as I stood absorbed in the loggers' technique:
"Have you ever seen a big tree fall?" "Yes."
"Good." Not the graceful faint we make
of tall trees in the mind,

but swift and shattering.
I counted the growth rings—one hundred sixty-four—
and found where, fifty years ago, the wood
drew in against the drought one narrow ring;
    I touched the band that marked the year
    when I was born, then stood

    and let them drop the rest.
This is everyday danger, mundane spectacle,
spectacular and dangerous all the same.
I hover between hope that it is practical
    to give young trees more light, and shame
    at laying old trees waste,

    then yank the starting cord
and turn to dropping stovewood from this chest-high limb,
my touch light, leaving real work to the saw,
my concentration thorough and ignored
    at once, lest the blade take on a whim
    of its own; and I think how

    our small towns have collected
in legend the curious deaths of ordinary men—
as once, on a siding up the road from here,
Jim Kaylor, if that was his name, directed
    the coupling of a single freight car
    to the middle of a train—

    an intricacy he knew
as most of us know how to shave, say, or shift gears.
That day, he managed to be caught somehow,
and the couplings clicked inside him, just below
    the ribcage, and he hung between cars
    in odd silence as the crew

    swarmed from the depot,
told each other to stand back, give him air, send
    for the doctor, and he asked for a cigarette,
received it with steady fingers, smoked, and saw—
    well, what could he have seen? The end
    of a boxcar, the set

of a face in disbelief,
or something, in smoke shapes before him, that he kept
    when he finished the cigarette, flicked it aside,
    nodded, and, as the boxcars were slipped
        apart, dropped with a sound of relief
        to the crossties, and died.

        Now I think hard for men
mangled by tractors and bulls, or crushed under trees
    that fall to ax or chainsaw in their season,
    and for myself, who for no particular reason
        so far survive, to watch the woodlot ease
        under the dark again,

        withdraw into the mist
of my unfocused eyes, into my waiting stare
    across bare trees that lift toward landscapes
    through which snakedoctors may still wheel to rest,
        then to walk home, behind the shapes
        my breath ghosts in sharp air.

One Morning, Shoeing Horses

I hold a shank while the blacksmith nails a shoe
in place, and think about how many years
I've worked at this—watching the horse's ears
for signs of what he might decide to do,
touching his neck, turning his head to coax
a little weight away from the lifted hoof,
the flywhisk light and always on the move,
the soothing whispers tuned to hammer strokes.

But I've been unsteady at it since a day
like this, some ten years back, when a driven nail
got under the blacksmith's wedding ring, unclinched.
There was a kind of roaring scream, the horse flinched
and snatched his hoof, and there the finger lay,
twitching a little, beside the water pail.

Two Husbands

1

She says she'll leave him if he screws around;
why not attempt it, if that's all it takes?
He fears forgiveness; through her, he has found
uprightness in his dreams of dodged mistakes.

2

The youthful urge to kill has left him dry,
that filled their first years with ecstatic woe;
he is content to wait, and watch things die:
as life goes on, he learns to let it go.

The Aging Professor Considers His Rectitude

There was something he had it on his mind to say
in class, a handsome catch of words that might have gone some way
toward explaining why, when he stood close to them,
he watched them surreptitiously, and waited for a hem
to rise. He pondered, too, the complex social laws
that he had wished to break, break like those men bred on applause
who drink their way from one small college to the next,
whose reputations burgeon as their eyes stray from the text
out to the breasts and suntanned knees in the third row.
Shopping the other day, he thought of it. He turned to go,
took up his groceries with a vague sweep of his arm,
and walked into the brilliant parking lot, his mind a swarm
of words and bits of words that winked out—like the stars?
No. More like blinding sunlight on the windows of parked cars. . . .
He would behave himself. He would not sidle up
to them before the weekly cinema, prepared to cup
a hand around a breast after the lights went down,
or else to take the attitude of a lascivious clown
whose very clownishness might let him get away
with saying, "How's about a little roll in yonder hay,
baby?" Somehow, he thought, he could explain all this
so they might feel how much he missed the things he chose to miss,
and think how noble his choice was. And then, they might . . .
too bad. Across the street, as he sat waiting for the light
to change, a boy was standing under the marquee
at the Home of the Whopper, catching a six-inch plastic E
at one end of a long aluminum shepherd's crook.
He watched the boy lift up the letter to its place, unhook
the pole, and slowly let it down to snag an A.
He almost had the hang of it. There went the final K.
The light turned green, and he turned right. The thought of STEAK,
as he drove home, gave way in time to how the rules might break
his way for once, if once the words would go his way.
His shepherd's crook somehow might catch a dream of making hay
long after sundown. In his narrow room, he changed
his shoes, unpacked his shopping bag. Slowly letters arranged
on cans of corn began to circle in his head
like some right words at some right time. They might somehow
　　be said.

Airing Linen

Wash and dry,
sort and fold:
you and I
are growing old.

Starting Over on an Old Ax

A shattered stroke, and then I heard him yell
"Shit fire!" I turned around in time to say
"Save matches!" as he flung the helve away,
then kicked the leaves awhile. "Now, where the hell
did the head get to?" I found it; we could tell
by what was in it just what kind of people
kept it tight: a wedge, wood screws, a fence staple,
a roofing tack, and one old hand-forged nail.
We dug and pulled, then stopped to drink a beer,
then wrestled it some more, piling the pieces
of junk between us on a stump. He said,
as he finished and held the reamed-out head
to one eye, like half a pair of field glasses,
"By God, partner, you can see from here to there."

Tradition and the Individual Talent

An old-school foxhunter let it get around
that he hunted a deer-proof pack. Hard to believe:
foxhounds are born to run foxes, all right,
but you have to make them stay off rabbits,
housecats, chickens, etc. They learn to stop
when the hound-whip cracks. Deer scent, though,
is strong enough to put whips out of their minds.

So, somebody asked, how do you do it?
Take a bag of deer scent and a hound,
put them both in a fifty-five-gallon oil drum,
and roll it down a hill or a rocky road.
God almighty. You claim this really works?
Seems to. One thing I'll say's for damn sure:
they stay away from fifty-five-gallon drums.

Kingston Trio, 1982

Nostalgia freaks unite. Our darkest fears
trot out on stage: Shane's gray, his voice is gone,
but substitutes for Guard and Reynolds clone
the sound that goes back almost thirty years.
Who *are* these guys? The grizzled, stoned crowd cheers
The Grand Reunion: Guard and Reynolds join
cracked voices to the rest, and decades run
through fingers fluffing riffs that no one hears.

This won't bring back a day in '61
when crowds outside a gym in Charlottesville
crushed to a door that none of us could see
sucking us through to hear how songs, until
they crack, can breed sweet hope that anyone
this time tomorrow reckons where he'll be.

Varieties of Religious Experience

This old day-worker, cleaning up
the grounds of an abandoned church,
getting ready to paint & put in glass,
said somebody from away from here
had bought it & was going to start
using it again. Well, it had been
a Methodist church, were these Methodists?
He believed it wasn't anybody like that,
no sir, he said; it is some of these
holy-sanctified God damn people.

Sick in Soul and Body Both

Bulls have small brains. I stood at the pipe fence
around my uncle's new concrete and steel
bull-pen and watched one of the residents
push his forehead against the pipes until
his front feet came up off the concrete walk
and all his weight was on that four-inch rail.
He spoke to me. It wasn't human talk,
but I could understand it pretty well.

That fence was tight, but I gave a quick salute
and came away from there. His brain was small,
but he knew one thing: all he wanted to do
was kill me. Men mean pain. And what I knew
was, it can work both ways. I wanted to shoot
that fucker, just to see him jump and fall.

The Last of the Emperor's Warriors

long seasons ago
there is no way to keep track
we scattered   each man

to his own jungle
I have grown into all that
remains of my clothes

now I crawl into
villages at night to find
garbage of famine

scour the jungle for
mouthfuls of bark   safe water
or edible snakes

silence in the leaves
poison waiting in the fruit
of survival's tree

the endless silence
of the enemy   I can
never stop thinking

of capture   I can
never surrender   not to
leaflets and bullhorns

preaching armistice
but it is hard when they sound
like my old father

not to give up now
his voice glances off the tree
I am hiding in

the shreds of my shoes
tremble as if they would lead
the way into light

but it is a trap
enemy voices whisper
from sheltering trees

they will come to me
on my own ground   there are more
of us than they know

Barbed Wire

One summer afternoon when nothing much
was happening, they were standing around
a tractor beside the barn while a horse
in the field poked his head between two strands
of the barbed-wire fence to get at the grass
along the lane, when it happened—something

they passed around the wood stove late at night
for years, but never could explain—someone
may have dropped a wrench into the toolbox
or made a sudden move, or merely thought
what might happen if the horse got scared, and
then he did get scared, jumped sideways and ran

down the fence line, leaving chunks of his throat
skin and hair on every barb for ten feet
before he pulled free and ran a short way
into the field, stopped and planted his hoofs
wide apart like a sawhorse, hung his head
down as if to watch his blood running out,

almost as if he were about to speak
to them, who almost thought he could regret
that he no longer had the strength to stand,
then shuddered to his knees, fell on his side,
and gave up breathing while the dripping wire
hummed like a bowstring in the splintered air.

III / At the Swings

The Muse Once More

I take the air, the sun,
my ease, letting things go for a while, as the dog
blunders from my feet to the curb and back.
The words in the book I am holding recede,
waver into illegibility; the air
trembles with jet planes, birds invade;
it is one of those days

when nothing at all
can go wrong. Across the way, I see my neighbor
lurching onto his lawn with some machine—
a rug shampooer? No, he straps a box
to his side, fastens earphones to his head,
and walks his lawn, sweeping before him
the sensitive disc

of a metal detector.
What in God's name is he looking for? It is ten-thirty;
he ought to be at work. But neither am I,
so I do not hail him. Back and forth,
back and forth he trudges over the spongy grass,
swinging the handle, his head cocked
for a signal whose meaning

I cannot guess. A lost
earring, perhaps, or the tap to the water meter;
no relics lie in this developed earth.
The sun moves higher overhead; he sweats,
walks on, and in my own head I begin
to carry that heavy intentness,
waiting for the whine

that will let me know
I have struck—what? The cars pass on their various
errands, snapping the asphalt bubbles,
and I doze here, dreaming that something lies
under a suburban lawn, waiting to change
my life, to draw me away from what
I chose too long ago

to forsake it now,
on some journey out of legend, to smuggle across

the world's best-guarded borders this token,
whatever it is, that says *I have risked
my life for this moment; do not forget me.
Whatever this makes me, accept it;
by this let me be known.*

And my neighbor walks on,
hunting the emblem that will tell him who he is now
or might once have become. I will not wait
to watch him find it; let it be the lost
treasure that turns his head on the pillow
as he drifts, as I do, toward sleep,
out of the life he has chosen.

To a Favorite Hostess

Someone on the verge of a kind of explosion
is trying to tell us a story, falling
toward silence and confusion,
now on the verge of saying, "Well,
you had to be there."

Then you come by with a tray
or a touch on the arm,
and we lift our glasses,
laugh, and square
our shoulders toward believing
that wherever we have to be,
we're always there.

Artichoke

If poetry did not exist, would you
have had the wit to invent it?
—HOWARD NEMEROV

He had studied in private years ago
the way to eat these things, and was prepared
when she set the clipped green globe before him.
He only wondered (as he always did
when he plucked from the base the first thick leaf,
dipped it into the sauce and caught her eye
as he deftly set the velvet curve against
the inside edges of his lower teeth
and drew the tender pulp toward his tongue
while she made some predictable remark
about the sensuality of this act
then sheared away the spines and ate the heart)
what mind, what hunger, first saw this as food.

Not Working

Whatever he was doing, he looks up
and stares past whatever there is—a lamp,
a window, trees, the shingled garden shed—
as if he were about to think of something
that might have happened to him once, and now
refuses to occur to him again.

He stares, then, doing absolutely nothing
for minutes, hours, or a whole afternoon,
as the lamp burns, and sunlight on the shed
brightens and fades; the trees put out their leaves
and let them fall, and seasons wear away
the days when what he wanted had a name.

Learning the Language

Tonight the windows hold
all light inside: they fold
it back on walls, and spill
gold over things that tell
us who we are. We hold
them in the corners of our eyes,
     playing a game
we have not tried to name:

half watched, half left alone,
the antique wood we own
takes on a life it learned
before our backs were turned:
when we are here alone,
the wood reverts to trees,
forests we garden in.
At first, the space between

the trees echoes with caution:
we coax them into motion,
familiar flowers rise,
old promises revise
themselves in whispered caution.
But then some gesture of the wind,
     a falling log
in the fire, a drift of fog

across the windowpane,
breathes toward some old refrain
we once had thought to speak.
Plainly the forest wakes;
now in the windowpane
flash quick reflections of light birds;
     a small wind sifts
among the trees and lifts

the undersides of leaves.
Imagined air unweaves
our losses and dissolves
ourselves into ourselves,
scatters us into leaves,

and you and I become
whatever words we may
have come so far to say.

Green Springs the Tree

My young son lurches halfway down the stair
or shrieks and totters midway through a climb
from the wobbling bookcase to the rocking chair.
I freeze and hold my breath. Most of the time
I am too far away to break the fall
that seldom comes. Instead, I stoop and bend
with him, as if threads of remote control
could reel out and connect him to my hand
that strains against his fall, against my leap
to rescue him. My twisting body prays
for skill in this, the high wire he will keep
both of us on as we rehearse the ways
to braid these strands of our inheritance
and teach poor body english how to dance.

Wineberries

That long afternoon I rode the grain binder,
one hand on the lever that raised and lowered
the knife as C.W. drove over the hills,

across ditches, rocks and spine-shattering holes,
my left foot strapped to a trip pedal lifted
every ten or twelve yards, over and over,

dropping sheaves, dropping sheaves, as if my whole life
lay ahead like a swath of ripe grain. This day
we were on the first round, opening the field

by an overgrown fence line, when C.W.
jumped off the tractor, dove into the briars,
and hollered, Great God, look at the wineberries!

I followed, and learned how the ripe ones, deep red,
fall to your palm at a touch, like raspberries,
but darker and scarcer—we could have eaten

forever, turning broad leaves to find clusters
ripening, safe from the blackbirds, in deep shade;
and C.W. told me how lucky we were—

how swiftly they ripen and shrivel away.
Now, many long stories later, my own house
stands in that field, the fence line still overgrown.

Toward midsummer I start watching the berries,
and one day I walk over there with my boys,
wanting to show them both something worth keeping.

The first ones I pick are bright red and stubborn,
not yet dark and heavy enough, and too sour.
But the boys know no more than I did; they crawl

in the brush to plunder the long hairy vines,
while I watch from the field's edge, the aftertaste
sharp on my tongue, wondering what ever happened

to C.W., or to the last day I stood
by the threshing machine, running the bagger,
not free to comb through the fence line; but by then

the wineberries were some weeks past their brief prime.

The Flying Change

1

The canter has two stride patterns, one on the right
lead and one on the left, each a mirror image of the
other. The leading foreleg is the last to touch the
ground before the moment of suspension in the air.
On cantered curves, the horse tends to lead with the
inside leg. Turning at liberty, he can change leads
without effort during the moment of suspension, but
a rider's weight makes this more difficult. The aim of
teaching a horse to move beneath you is to remind
him how he moved when he was free.

2

A single leaf turns sideways in the wind
in time to save a remnant of the day;
I am lifted like a whipcrack to the moves
I studied on that barbered stretch of ground,
before I schooled myself to drift away

from skills I still possess, but must outlive.
Sometimes when I cup water in my hands
and watch it slip away and disappear,
I see that age will make my hands a sieve;
but for a moment the shifting world suspends

its flight and leans toward the sun once more,
as if to interrupt its mindless plunge
through works and days that will not come again.
I hold myself immobile in bright air,
sustained in time astride the flying change.

Projectile Point, Circa 2500 B.C.

In the garden in high summer as the sun dropped,
I worked my hoe in short scythe-swings
until one stroke turned a pebble I stopped to pick up.
I stood pinching it, thumbing off earth crumbs;

this has happened before, but not to me.
There were dozens of these in a black japanned box
in my grandfather's bedroom, which was also
his grandfather's bedroom. In the days when men

plowed the fields behind horses, sunup to sundown
watching the furrow open up and lie over,
three paces ahead of their feet, there was time
to reach down midstride and pocket a recognized stone.

At such times a man might fall to imagining,
but why not stick to such facts as may be?
It is broken at tip and base: botched,
chipped at the end of a shaft-flight,

or lost until it broke under the plow;
and such facts as there are now include
one hot afternoon when I stood sole-deep
in soft ground, wondering at the four thousand years

between the two men who had touched this stone,
guessing how it was not to care
for the magic I felt flowing out of it,
but just to stand here, touching only an implement

like a hoe or a pitchfork, watching the ground
as I watched it, not thinking of the sun
moving on as it moved over me, as it will
when the rocks and the water are alone here again.

Hawk

Last year I learned to speak to a red-tail hawk.
He wheeled above me as I crossed a field;
he screamed; I pulled a blade of grass, set it
against my lips, and started screaming back.

We held that conversation for half a mile.
Once in a while he calls me out of the house
and I comb a border for the right blade of grass.
I used to wish I might learn what it is

we mean to one another; now, I keep
the noise we've mastered for itself alone,
for glimpses of his descent toward dead elms,
and a heart that will not mind when I am gone.

Not Yet

The day may come when I will sit in a chair and stare
    myself slowly away,
or stand still at the edge of a field or the end
    of an unfamiliar street
grappling for the memory that might seem to make long
    life worthwhile,

but today, almost dozing in noon sun, I blinked and
    looked down the driveway
in time to see six deer come over the fence out of
    nowhere, their sharp feet
barely printing the ground, and melt into woods
    toward absolute purity of style.

At the Swings

Midafternoon in Norfolk,
late July. I am taking our two sons for a walk
away from their grandparents' house; we have
directions to a miniature playground,
and I have plans to wear them down
toward a nap at five,

when my wife and I
will leave them awhile with her father. A few blocks
south of here, my wife's mother drifts from us
beneath hospital sheets, her small strength bent
to the poisons and the rays they use
against a spreading cancer.

In their house now, deep love
is studying to live with deepening impatience
as each day gives our hopes a different form
and household tasks rise like a powdery mist
of restless fatigue. Still, at five,
my wife and I will dress

and take the boulevard
across the river to a church where two dear friends
will marry; rings will be blessed, promises kept
and made, and while our sons lie down to sleep,
the groom's niece, as the flower girl,
will almost steal the show.

But here the boys have made
an endless procession on the slides, shrieking down
slick steel almost too hot to touch; and now
they charge the swings. I push them from the front,
one with each hand, until at last
the rhythm, and the sunlight

that splashes through live oak
and crape myrtle, dappling dead leaves on the ground,
lull me away from this world toward a state
still and remote as an old photograph
in which I am standing somewhere
I may have been before:

there was this air, this light,
a day of thorough and forgetful happiness;
    where was it, or how long ago? I try
    to place it, but it has gone for good,
        to leave me gazing at these swings,
            thinking of something else

        I may have recognized—
an irrecoverable certainty that now,
    and now, this perfect afternoon, while friends
    are struggling to put on their cutaways
        or bridal gowns, and my wife's mother,
            dearer still, is dozing

            after her medicine,
or turning a small thing in her mind, like someone
    worrying a ring of keys to make small sounds
    against great silence, and while these two boys
        swing back and forth against my hand,
            time's crosshairs quarter me

            no matter where I turn.
Now it is time to go. The boys are tired enough,
    and my wife and I must dress and go to church.
    Because I love our friends, and ceremony,
        the usual words will make me weep:
            hearing the human prayers

        for holy permanence
will remind me that a life is much to ask
    of anyone, yet not too much to give
    to love. And once or twice, as I stand there,
        that dappled moment at the swings
            will rise between the lines,

        when I beheld our sons
as, in the way of things, they will not be again,
    though even years from now their hair may lift
    a little in the breeze, as if they stood
        somewhere along their way from us,
            poised for a steep return.